LET CHRIST BE MAGNIFIED

Calvin's Teaching for Today

J. H. MERLE D'AUBIGNÉ

Time exists to show Christ's glory
— CALVIN

THE BANNER OF TRUTH TRUST

THE BANNER OF TRUTH TRUST
3 Murrayfield Road, Edinburgh EH12 6EL, UK
P.O. Box 621, Carlisle, PA 17013, USA

*

First published in London, 1864,
as *Calvin's Teaching for the Present Day*

First Banner of Truth edition, 2007
© Banner of Truth Trust, 2007

ISBN-13: 978 0 85151 959 3

*

Typeset in 11.5/16 pt Sabon at the
Banner of Truth Trust, Edinburgh
Printed in the USA by
Versa Press, Inc.,
East Peoria, IL

LET CHRIST BE MAGNIFIED
Calvin's Teaching for Today

'So now also Christ shall be magnified
in my body, whether it be
by life or by death.'

PHILIPPIANS 1:20

CONTENTS

PUBLISHER'S PREFACE

O<small>N</small> 27 M<small>AY</small> 1564, John Calvin, 'servant of the Word of God in the church of Geneva', passed to his eternal reward. Exactly three hundred years later, Dr J. H. Merle d'Aubigné, the famous historian of the Reformation, stood up to address a large gathering in the same city on 'Calvin's Teaching for the Present Day'.

In the years that have passed since, Calvin's reputation and influence as the foremost systematic theologian and Bible commentator of the Reformation era, and one of the greatest in all the Christian centuries, have continued to grow. But even in a time when detailed and scholarly discussions of virtually every aspect of the Reformer's work and thought abound, Merle d'Aubigné's testimony to the grand, central themes of Calvin's teaching remains of outstanding value.

Who was the distinguished speaker on 27 May 1864? Jean Henri Merle d'Aubigné (1794–1872),[1] the most popular church historian of the nineteenth century, was born on 16 August 1794 into a well-known Huguenot family in Geneva.

In 1685 Louis XIV of France revoked the Edict of Nantes, which had protected French Protestants from persecution. Thousands fled France, including the paternal great-grandfather of Jean Henri, Jean Louis Merle, who escaped from Nîmes to Geneva.

In the middle of the following century, Francis Merle, the son of Jean Louis, married Elizabeth d'Aubigné, a descendant of the famous poet and historian, Theodore Agrippa d'Aubigné (1552–1630). The children of this union all retained their mother's maiden name, adopting Merle

---

[1] The Trust publishes *The Reformation in England* in two volumes (London: Banner of Truth, 1962, often reprinted). The contents of this volume were extracted from Merle d'Aubigné's two major multi-volume histories (see pp. xv–xvi below).

d'Aubigné as the family name. The historian was the second son of Aimé Robert Merle d'Aubigné, and the grandson of Francis and Elizabeth.

Jean Henri soon showed an academic bent and entered the Academy of Geneva. After completing an Arts course, he moved on to the Faculty of Theology. The influence of Calvin's theology had long departed from Geneva, and had been replaced by a stifling Unitarianism. D'Aubigné recorded that in his four years of theological study in the Academy, 'not one hour was consecrated to the study of Holy Scripture'. The sources most cited were not Christ and the apostles but Plato, Cicero, and Seneca.

It was into this apparently unpromising scene that a true theological heir of Calvin and of the Reformation, the Scotsman Robert Haldane,[1] entered in 1816. Haldane (1764–1842) had been engaged in a missionary tour of France and Switzerland and was about to leave Geneva when a

[1] See Alexander Haldane, *The Lives of Robert and James Haldane*, 1852; repr. Edinburgh: Banner of Truth, 1990, especially pp. 413–62, and Robert Haldane's *Romans* (1874; repr. London: Banner of Truth, 1958, often reprinted).

seemingly chance encounter led him to invite the theology students of Geneva to his apartments to study the Bible.

Between twenty and thirty students, including Merle d'Aubigné, responded to the invitation, to the great irritation of their professor who 'made it his business to pace up and down under the shady trees of the avenue at the time the students were assembling, making clear his high displeasure at their attendance, and noting their names in his pocket book'. D'Aubigné describes Haldane's influence on him in this way:[1]

I met Robert Haldane and heard him read from an English Bible a chapter from Romans about the natural corruption of man, a doctrine of which I had never before heard. In fact I was quite astonished to hear of man being corrupt by nature. I remember saying to Mr Haldane, 'Now I see that doctrine in the Bible.' 'Yes,' he replied, 'but do you see it in your heart?' That was but a simple question, yet it came home to my conscience. It was the sword of the Spirit:

[1] See also p. 16 below.

and from that time I saw that my heart was corrupted, and knew from the Word of God that I can be saved by grace alone. So that, if Geneva gave something to Scotland at the time of the Reformation, if she communicated light to John Knox, Geneva has received something from Scotland in return in the blessed exertions of Robert Haldane.

Haldane's brief stay in Geneva greatly strengthened *le Réveil*, the Awakening in the city which appears to have lasted till 1830. In later years, d'Aubigné would point to the apartments that Haldane had once occupied, saying, 'There is the cradle of the second Genevan Reformation.'

In July 1817, d'Aubigné was ordained a minister of the established church in Geneva, but he did not then enter the pastorate, choosing rather to travel widely through the German-speaking lands before continuing his studies in the University of Berlin. In the autumn of 1817 he attended the tercentenary celebrations at the Wartburg Castle, near Eisenach, of Martin Luther's *Ninety-five Theses*.

What struck him most forcefully at these celebrations was that it was essentially Luther's intellectual and political significance that was being highlighted; his spiritual significance appeared to have been forgotten. It was then, at the age of 23, that d'Aubigné resolved to write a history of the Reformation that would emphasize the religious significance of the whole movement.

'I want this history to be truly Christian,' he wrote, 'and to give a proper impulse to the religious spirit.'

In June 1818, d'Aubigné assumed the pastorate of the French Reformed Church in Hamburg which had been established by French Huguenots fleeing from their homeland during the persecution under Louis XIV. He remained in this pastorate until 1823 when he received an invitation from King Willem I of the Netherlands to become the pastor of a French- and German-speaking church in Brussels. His ministry in Brussels appears to have been more influential than that in Hamburg. Many from the court attended his church, as did King Willem himself, with his Prussian wife, Wilhelmina Frederika, as well as Guillaume Groen van Prinsterer, the royal historian and author of *Unbelief and Revolution*. D'Aubigné held this post in Brussels until the Revolution of 1830, which led to the separation of Belgium from Holland. After seeking to help the scattered members of his congregation during the crisis, he decided to leave Brussels in June 1831 in order to accept an invitation to help establish a theological seminary in Geneva. He was appointed Professor of Church History there, and was joined shortly afterwards by Louis Gaussen, later famous as the author of a significant work on the plenary inspiration of the Scriptures. Merle d'Aubigné remained at the seminary until his death in 1872.

The resolution that he had made in 1817 came to fruition during the forty-one years spent as professor in Geneva. In this time he visited the major libraries of Central and Western Europe to read original documents in Latin, French, German, Dutch, and English. In 1835 the first volume of *The History of the Reformation of the Sixteenth Century* was published in French. The five-volume work was completed in 1853. This was followed by *The History of the Reformation in Europe in the Time of Calvin* in eight volumes, published in French between 1863 and 1878, the last three volumes appearing posthumously.

The immense popularity of the *History* is evident from the remark of the church historian Philip Schaff that this work 'had a wider circulation, at least in the English translations, than any other book on church history'.

The principal factor in its popularity is the powerful personal element that pervades the work. The author focuses on the lives of men such as Luther, Melanchthon, Zwingli, Farel, Calvin, Tyndale, Cranmer, and many others whose names are less well known. He recounts their struggles, their labours, their sufferings, their failures, their triumphs, and their Christian heroism. It is undoubtedly this emphasis which lends vividness and interest to his writing of history.

The second major factor in his popularity is the powerful divine element that pervades his writing. He wrote that the historian 'ought to embrace in his survey the whole field of human affairs. He must, of course, take into consideration the earthly powers that bear sway in the world, ambition, despotism, liberty; but he ought to mark also the heavenly powers which religion reveals. The living God must not be excluded from the world which He created.'

'There is in history,' he wrote, 'as in the body, a soul.' It was the soul of the grand drama of the sixteenth century that Merle d'Aubigné sought to lay bare. He did not write as a detached, disinterested spectator; he loved the Reformation of the sixteenth century, for he saw in it a mighty movement of the Spirit of God, unparalleled since the early days of Christianity.

The same warmth pervades the account he gives in the pages that follow of the essential features of Calvin's teaching.

* * * * *

The tercentenary of Calvin's death on 27 May 1864 was the occasion of the commencement of the first tangible monument in Geneva to the memory of the Reformer, briefly alluded to in Merle d'Aubigné's address.[1] Calvin himself had not wished even a stone to mark his grave. But now on d'Aubigné's initiative, and with the support of the international Evangelical Alliance, the construction of a large hall known as the 'Calvinium' or 'Salle de la Réformation' was begun. Opened in 1867, the hall played a major role in the religious and cultural life of Geneva for a century, even hosting the annual assemblies of the League of Nations during the 1920s. It was demolished in 1969.[2]

[1] See pp. 2–3 below.
[2] The history of the building is described in *Croire à Genève: La Salle de la Réformation, XIX–XX siècles* (Geneva: Labor et Fides, 2006).

OUTLINE OF CALVIN'S LIFE

JOHN CALVIN (in French, *Cauvin*) was born in
Noyon in Picardy, about sixty miles north-
east of Paris, on 10 July 1509. He was the
second son of Gérard Cauvin, an official in the
service of the bishop of Noyon.

Destined by his father for a career in the
Church, John was given ecclesiastical benefices
and sent to Paris at about fourteen years of age
to study at the University. He first attended the
Collège de la Marche, then the Collège de
Montaigu, where he received a Master of Arts
degree in 1528.

In this formative period, his associations with
the brilliant Latin scholar Mathurin Cordier,
with his cousin Pierre Robert Olivétan, who was

already attracted to Lutheran teaching, and with the family of Guillaume Cop, Physician to the King of France, were signficant pointers to the future.

On the conclusion of Calvin's studies at Montaigu, his father directed him to study for the more lucrative profession of Law. Accordingly he went first to the University of Orléans (1528–9), then to the University of Bourges (1529–31), where he studied with some of the most eminent jurists of the time. He also pursued his literary interests and studied Greek under the learned Lutheran scholar Melchior Wolmar. On the death of his father in 1531, Calvin abandoned the study of Law to devote himself entirely to literary scholarship. Returning to Paris, he attended the new Collège de France, founded by the King and, in 1532, published his first work, a commentary on Seneca's *De Clementia*.

Sometime in late 1533 or early 1534, he experienced the turning point he later described as his 'sudden conversion'. In the Preface to his *Commentary on the Psalms* he wrote:

I was withdrawn from the study of philosophy, and was put to the study of law. To this pursuit I endeavoured faithfully to apply myself, in obedience to the will of my father; but God, by the secret guidance of his providence, at length gave a different direction to my course. And first, since I was too obstinately addicted to the superstitions of Popery to be easily extricated from so profound an abyss of mire, God by a sudden conversion subdued and brought my mind to a teachable frame, which was more hardened in such matters than might have been expected from one at my early period of life.

This event has been linked with an address delivered by his friend Nicholas Cop, Rector of the University of Paris, on All Saints' Day, 1533. The address advocated reform of the Church, using language borrowed from Luther and Erasmus. This provoked speedy action by the authorities against Cop and others believed to be tainted with heresy. Many thought that Calvin was the real author of the address. He fled Paris for a time, returned briefly, then left once more. Seeking refuge with his friend Louis du Tillet in Angoulême, he came to the decision to break with the old Church and devote himself to the cause of reform. In May 1534 he resigned his benefices at Noyon and, towards the end of that year or early in 1535, as measures against Protestants became increasingly severe, he left France and sought a haven in Protestant Basle.

There he made contact with the Reformers in Strasbourg and in Switzerland and in March 1536 published the first edition of his *Institutes of the Christian Religion*, prefaced with a letter to the King of France, Francis I, defending the beliefs of the persecuted French Protestants.

He returned briefly to France to settle some family business, then in June set out for Strasbourg. Finding the most direct route blocked by military operations he stopped for the night in Geneva. He was recognized. William Farel, leader of the Genevan Reformation, hearing that the author of the *Institutes* was in the city, pleaded for Calvin's help. Calvin insisted that he was seeking seclusion for quiet study. Farel did his best to detain him, and finally declared that if he did not stay in Geneva, God would curse his peace. 'By this imprecation', Calvin wrote, 'I was so stricken with terror, that I desisted from the journey which I had undertaken. I felt as if God had laid his mighty hand on me to arrest me.' Calvin quickly rose to a position of leadership alongside Farel. From now till his death in 1564, Geneva was to be the main scene of his labours.

Increasing friction between the two Reformers and the city authorities over the ordering and discipline of the church eventually led to Calvin and Farel being ordered to leave Geneva in April 1538. But the exile was temporary. Calvin was recalled to the city in September 1541.

The intervening period, spent in Strasbourg, was fruitful. At Martin Bucer's invitation, Calvin became pastor of a church consisting mainly of French refugees, lectured in theology, published a second edition of the *Institutes* (1539) and a commentary on Romans (1539), and in 1540 married Idelette de Bure. She died in 1549, and all three of their children died in infancy.

Following his recall to Geneva, Calvin's new constitution for the city's church, the *Ecclesiastical Ordinances*, was accepted in November 1541. But struggles over church discipline continued for most of the rest of Calvin's life, and the right to excommunicate was only conceded in 1555. Opposition to Calvin, spearheaded by the party known as the Libertines, also continued till the same year. In fact, despite such episodes as the execution of Michael Servetus in 1553, discussed by Merle d'Aubigné below,[1] Geneva remained a republic, not a theocracy, and Calvin's influence was mainly exerted through preaching.

Especially in the latter years of Calvin's life, the reputation of the city as the fountainhead of reform and the centre of a movement of international scope continued to grow. Refugees flocked to Geneva, which was widely seen as the major 'city of refuge'. Efforts were also made to evangelize other lands, particularly France.

Despite recurring ill-health, frequent preaching, constant requests for help and advice, and

[1] See pp. 7–8.

numerous distractions, Calvin's literary output was immense. In addition to the *Institutes*,[1] theological and polemical works, and published sermons, commentaries were published on most of the books of the Bible.[2]

Calvin preached for the last time on 6 February 1564. On Easter Sunday he went to church for the last time, singing with the rest of the congregation at the conclusion, 'Lord, now lettest thou thy servant depart in peace . . . for mine eyes have seen thy salvation.' On 25 April he dictated his will and final testimony,[3] and on 27 May he entered into his eternal reward.

THE PUBLISHER
May 2007

[1] Further Latin editions appeared in 1543, 1550 and 1559, with French translations by Calvin himself in 1545, 1551 and 1560.

[2] For a list of Calvin titles published by the Banner of Truth Trust, see p. 53 below.

[3] See *Letters of John Calvin* (Edinburgh: Banner of Truth, 1980), p. 29.

JOHN CALVIN
A Biographical Table

1509 (10 July)	Birth of Calvin
1528	Graduates Master of Arts, Paris
1528–9	Studies Law at Orléans
1529–31	Studies Law at Bourges
1532	*Commentary on De Clementia*
1533 (1 Nov)	Nicholas Cop's Rectoral Address
1533–4 (Winter)	Conversion
1534–5 (Winter)	Leaves France for Basle
1536 (March)	First edition of *Institutes*
1536 (June)	Meets Farel in Geneva
1538 (April)	Exiled to Strasbourg
1539	Second edition of *Institutes*; *Commentary on Romans*
1540 (Aug)	Marries Idelette de Bure
1541 (Sept)	Recalled to Geneva
1541 (Nov)	*Ecclesiastical Ordinances* accepted
1549 (April)	Death of Idelette
1553 (Oct)	Servetus executed
1555	End of Libertines' opposition; right to excommunicate conceded
1559	Final edition of *Institutes*
1559	Founding of the Geneva Academy
1564 (6 Feb)	Last sermon
1564 (27 May)	Death of Calvin

LET CHRIST BE MAGNIFIED

INTRODUCTION

WE FEEL A TRUE CHRISTIAN JOY at the sight of the brethren who, for the sake of this glorious anniversary, have come from the other cantons of Switzerland, from France and Germany, Belgium and Holland, England and Ireland, Italy and elsewhere, to render their united thanks to God for the good he has done their churches and their countries through the ministry of the great Reformer. We also feel emotions of gratitude to the Lord at the sight of the numerous Christians of this city who remember the temporal and spiritual benefits which they and their families have received, and are still receiving, from God, through our blessed

Reformation. Our first thought is, therefore, to bless the thrice-holy God. 'Alleluia! Salvation, and glory, and honour, and power, unto the Lord our God' (*Rev.* 19:1).

But our second thought is this, that at the very outset of this commemoration we should reject every idea of honouring the Reformer beyond what is fitting, and we know that you join with us in this. Nothing was so offensive to Calvin as the folly of those who exalted him: 'They wanted to make an idol of me', he said, 'and of Geneva a Jerusalem.'[1]

Were we to give him any honour beyond what is due to one who has loved God and served him faithfully, but who was still a man, he would say to us, in his own words: 'Beware of so doing. The honour due to God alone is profaned as soon as men ascribe the smallest portion whatsoever of it to the creature.'

The monument[2] whose first spiritual stone we have laid this morning, with prayers and in the

[1] *Lettres Françaises*, I, p. 351.
[2] This relates to the 'Calvinium' or 'Salle de la Réformation', a hall whose construction was begun in 1864 on the initiative of d'Aubigné. See pp. xvi and xvii above.

Lord's presence, shall, with God's help, bear these words of the Reformer: 'Let us give honour to persons who excel in the fear of God, but on condition that God remains above all, and that Christ triumphs.'

Yet if we abstain from idle eulogy, if we refuse to canonize John Calvin, must we then be silent? Must we not give to every man his due? If this very year [1864] the tercentenaries of Galileo and of Shakespeare have been celebrated with so much solemnity, doubtless, without any idea of making saints of them (and strange saints indeed they would be!), I do not know why we should not modestly call to mind that great teacher of the Scriptures of God, who has undeniably exercised upon the destinies of Christianity, and on the civilization of the world, a very different influence from that of the greatest poets or the most illustrious men of science.

There is a special obligation on us to do it, for there is perhaps no person in history more misunderstood than he. We see him continually exposed, even in this day, to the poisoned arrows proceeding from two extreme parties. And shall we keep silence, we who are amazed by these falsehoods? No! At such a moment as this, ingratitude must not be counted among the virtues of a Christian. 'Open your mouth for the dumb', says Scripture. Is he not dumb, he whose mortal frame has lain in the dust these three hundred years?

Calvin has been represented as a hard man, devoid of natural affection — yet rarely has husband or father uttered more affecting cries than those he uttered at the death of his wife and of his children.[1]

He has been represented as a gloomy, un-sociable man, who certainly would not, like Jesus, have been present at the marriage feast at Cana; and yet he wrote to a friend, in 1548, on the occasion of a marriage: 'As for the wedding, I hope we shall have a good one. There must be company invited, though not a crowd.'[2]

He has been represented as a narrow-minded, bigoted sectarian; and yet all his life was spent

[1] Letters to Viret and to Farel, 7th and 11th April, 1549.

[2] *Lettres Françaises*, I, p. 255.

in attempts to draw the Christians and churches of the Protestant world closer together.

Still, it is nonetheless true, we are told, that he opposed and combatted all who entertained opinions different from his. Replying to the Queen of Navarre, who had reproached him on this point, he said: 'A dog barks when he sees his master attacked, and shall I be dumb and utter not a word, when my Lord and my God is attacked?'[1]

Yet Calvin was a man, and there is no man that has not fallen into error. His capital error was one that was universal in the sixteenth century.

Under the Old Testament dispensation God spoke to a people. He gave his commandments to Israel; the law of the people constrained transgressors to obey him who was their King. But under the New Testament dispensation, God speaks individually to the souls ransomed by the blood of Christ in every people and nation, which he gathers out and forms into the assembly and church of the living God.

---

[1] *Lettres Françaises,* I, p. 114.

The Lord is not willing to have any longer a special nation, inhabiting a certain country. He has established no new theocracy, either at Jerusalem or at Rome, in London, Amsterdam, or Geneva. This is a fact that Calvin did not clearly recognize. Assuredly he never desired to make an 'idol' of himself; but it seems that he wished in some degree to make a 'Jerusalem' of Geneva.

It was a noble error. God, who is continually extracting good from evil, blessed the foundation of a Christian republic. In the sixteenth century a refuge for the persecuted was needed, a shrine where the holy fire should be preserved, from where the life-giving light should continually pour forth its rays. The church which was *deformed* had its centre in Rome; the church which was *reformed* was also to have its centre, and that it found in Geneva.

Without this concentration and powerful unity, the new system of light, of morality, and of liberty, would have encountered formidable dangers. Geneva became the European capital of a great opinion. And yet the attempt produced unhappy results. While the magistrates believed themselves, according to the principles of Roman Catholicism, called to punish heresy as a crime, Calvin, impelled, doubtless, by higher motives, desired to prevent the contagion from spreading, to prevent its tainting the divine life, and compromising the existence of the people of God.[1]

But on a memorable occasion, when the Reformation was threatened, not only at Geneva, but elsewhere, by doctrines which would have paralysed the regenerating movement, Calvin (and in this he stood alone) entreated the judges to modify the penalty.[2] He conjured them not to condemn Servetus to the stake.[3] It was, alas! of no effect; a deplorable mistake was committed. We must confess that Calvin had his share, too great a share, in the general error: he should have

---

[1] *Ne longius maneret contagio* (that the contagion may no longer remain). Calvin to Sulzer, 8 September 1553.

[2] *Pœnæ atrocitatem remitti cupio* (I desire to reduce the severity of the penalty). Calvin to Farel, 20 August 1553.

[3] *Genus mortis conati sumus mutare, sed frustra* (We attempted to change the manner of death, but in vain). Calvin to Farel, 28 October 1553.

been above his age. It was the action of the civil power against heresy which compromised evangelical doctrine in Geneva, and which, even to this day, foments prejudices and inspires declamatory abuse against the Reformer. We reject this error. There is no longer a Jerusalem, and there cannot be one. We desire the truth, but we desire it in liberty.

We have not come here, however, to speak of Calvin in his political and social aspects. We have no wish to set him before you as the man who (possibly without any such anticipation) has done the most for modern civilization. Let our witnesses be the Calvinistic nations of our day, where general prosperity and liberty flourish more than anywhere else. Our object is purely religious.

We have sought for the characteristic feature of this great Christian personality. Is it the recognition of the sovereignty of God, absolute submission to his will, the organization of the church? The first of these features is the most prominent; and yet we must mount still higher to find the key of his doctrine and of his life. *Excelsior!* Higher, and higher still! This was

Calvin's motto: his soul perpetually soared towards heaven. The glory of God, the glory of Christ; this was his overruling idea, the principle of his activity, the aim of his whole life.

From the time when Paul said, 'Christ shall be magnified in my body, whether it be by life or by death', no man, perhaps, has been able to repeat these words with more truth than our Reformer. *LET CHRIST BE MAGNIFIED!* This is what he requires of churches, believers, and martyrs. When he wrote to the imprisoned ladies of Paris,[1] who were about to die at the stake, he said to them, almost literally repeating the Apostle's words: 'For this we were brought into the world, and enlightened by God's grace, that we should magnify him in our life and in our death.'

All Calvin's life proclaimed, glory, glory, glory to Christ, and to self confusion of face. Glory to his *Word,* glory to his *Person,* glory to his *Grace,* glory to his *Life.* These are the four 'glories' which both the Apostle and the Reformer invite you to render to the Lord.

[1] Mesdames de Graveron, de Champagne, etc. *Lettres Françaises,* II, p. 145.

You will easily understand why, at the present epoch, we cling to this thought. You are not such strangers in Jerusalem that you know not the things which are happening in these days. 'Now', to employ the Reformer's language, 'now is the time to bring to light the glory of Jesus Christ.'[1]

And who can do it better than himself? He reappears (so to speak) as the teacher of the present generation; he speaks to the present time and deserves our attention. For we are hesitating, and he is firm; we are superficial, and he is profound; we have extreme consideration for ourselves, and he sacrificed himself to God daily. Let us listen, then, to the ancient doctor who comes back from the grave to speak to us and, like him, *let us magnify Christ.*

[1] *Commentary on John* 2:11.

I

CHRIST'S WORD

CHRIST'S GOSPEL is what Calvin, the doctor of ancient as well as of modern times, glorified foremost in his life. The Reformer was not willing to select among the traditions of men, and to preserve the least anti-scriptural; he put them all aside, to set up in their place the Word of God only. Let all the idols of men perish, and let Christ's glory remain alone. That was the great mainspring of his life.

At Lausanne, at the time of the celebrated discussion;[1] at Geneva, and everywhere, he refused to acknowledge the authority of the

[1] At a synod in Lausanne in July 1538, Calvin refused to put the authority of the creeds above the Scriptures.

church and of the ancient councils (which had, however, generally professed Christian truth), and defended the exclusive and regulating authority of Scripture. He proclaimed it alike in the presence of sceptical reason and of a superstitious church. He is for the Bible, the whole Bible, and nothing but the Bible. 'Woe to the Papists', he said, 'who have no other rule of faith than the tradition of the Church. As for us, let us remember that the Son of God, who alone can and ought to pronounce in this matter, approves of no other faith but that which comes from the doctrine of the Apostles, of which we find no certain testimony except in their writings.'[1]

And how could he resist exalting the Word of God? When Calvin was yet a fervent Catholic, and studying at the Montaigu College in Paris — when, troubled in conscience, he sought, but sought in vain, to quiet it by confessing his sins to the priests — what was it that rescued him from his anguish? Scripture, nothing but Holy Scripture. 'O Lord!' he exclaimed — and we

[1] *Commentary on John* 17:20.

Christ's Word

quote his very words — 'You have enlightened me with the brightness of your Spirit. You have put your Word as a lamp to my feet. The clouds which before now veiled your glory have been dispelled by it, and the blessings of your Anointed have shone clearly upon my eyes. What I have learnt from your mouth (that is to say, from your Word) I will distribute faithfully to your church.'[1] From this moment Calvin is full of admiration for Christ and his Word; he is jealous of the glory of Holy Scripture. He will not have its purity soiled by imputing to it any error, or its beauty hidden by throwing over it the veils of any human system. Glory, glory to the Word of God!

This is a vital feature in the Reformer of Geneva. Luther had dwelt upon the human element in the Bible, and on the human differences among the books that compose it. Even while acknowledging and proclaiming it as the divine Word, he had perhaps exaggerated

[1] Letter to Cardinal Jacopo Sadoleto, reprinted in *A Reformation Debate*, ed. J. C. Olin, Fordham University Press, 2000; also in *Calvin's Tracts relating to the Reformation*, vol. 1, Calvin Translation Society, 1844, repr. Baker Book House and other publishers.

supposed anomalies; as the shades of difference between James and Paul, between Moses and Christ. Calvin specially upheld the divine element in Scripture, the absolute inspiration of the Word, and the grand unity resulting therefrom. 'The principle which distinguishes our religion from all others', he said (and modern Protestants should listen attentively to his words) 'is the knowledge we possess that God has spoken to us.'[1] He did not overlook the human element: he declared that the holy men of God were not 'beside themselves, as the pagans said of their prophets'; but he added that they did not put forward at random the truth we have received written by their hands: they only proclaimed what they had received from on high.[2]

This is a mere theological question, you may say; and then turn away. A theological question, if you wish to call it so; but observe — for it is a matter which concerns you — that it is pre-eminently a practical question, one of individual salvation.

[1] *Commentary on 2 Timothy* 3:16.
[2] *Commentary on 2 Peter* 1:20.

The Word of God is the only power that can subdue the rebellion of our heart. There is a power in our fallen nature which revolts against divine truth, and which nothing human can overcome. No teaching of man will do it, not even that of your father or your mother. The teaching of the church and of the most beloved pastors will not do it, nor time-worn tradition, which is the teaching of the ages. All this is as powerless as the slenderest thread to lift the weight which presses us down. To make the kingdom of God enter our hearts we need a battering-ram that can overthrow the strongest walls, and that ram is the Word of God.

We remember the time of the first Revival.[1] The period of our struggles — and they were often fierce struggles — is still before us; and we declare that our resistance was only surmounted

---

[1] The reference is to *le Réveil,* a movement of the Spirit of God which began in Geneva in 1816–7 through the ministry of Robert Haldane. Haldane is the 'venerable Christian' referred to on p. 16. See also Alexander Haldane, *The Lives of Robert and James Haldane*, 1852; repr. Edinburgh: Banner of Truth, 1990, pp. 413–62, and pp. xi–xiii above.

by the clear and infallible Word of God. The idea of original sin, for instance, of a corruption innate and hereditary in man, irritated our pride, and opposed our ideas about the purity of the human heart: we rejected it with disdain. And how was our obstinacy vanquished? One day a venerable Christian opened the Epistle to the Romans before us. We looked at the book, and, among other declarations, read these words: 'By one man sin entered into the world.' Whereupon, unable to resist the testimony of God, we exclaimed, 'Yes; now we see original sin in the Bible!' At these words, the friend who had shown us this declaration in Scripture, pointed to our breast, and asked, solemnly, 'Do you see it in your heart?' O God! it was then you made us to see it. Your Spirit unveiled it before us. Your Word pierced our heart more sharply than a two-edged sword; and, convinced of sin, we fell at your feet, and cried, 'Save, O Lord, save us by the grace of Jesus Christ!'

The Word had then great power: is it so in our days? It must increase. Holy Scripture is a torch which enlightens continually — a sword never blunted. Men vainly strive to rob it of its heavenly splendour; they could sooner strip the sun of its light. Ministers of the gospel, and disciples of Jesus Christ, exalt and magnify, all of you, the Word of your Master. Hold it high in your hearts, but bring it down to the lowliest soul. Hear what the great teacher of the sixteenth century says, on the anniversary of his death, to the present generation:

> The Word of God teaches so clearly, that it enlightens at the first glance. It must penetrate to the very bottom of your hearts. It is not enough to feel a few slight stings and pricks; you must be wounded, pierced through and through by the Word; and your old man must be killed by the edge of this spiritual sword.[1]

The divine oracles are the principle of life.

The Reformation overthrew the authority of Papal Bulls and scholastic logic, only to set in their place the authority of the Word of God. This is its fundamental principle. If we reject it,

[1] *Commentary on Hebrews* 4:12.

as the new doctors would have us, Protestantism has no foundation. It will fall either, on the one hand, into Popery, Jesuitry, and slavery, or, on the other, into Deism, Pantheism, Atheism, and Libertinism; but fall it must. Stop, you destroyers! Restrain your hands, you who attack the divinity of the Word! If you continue your work, and if God should permit it to succeed, you would destroy all the elements of light, life, liberty, and holiness that are in the world.

But we do not fear. The divine Word will continue as the supreme authority in which we must believe, and as the divine well-spring from which we can draw the waters of life. Cease, then, your useless contests; recognize your strange delusion. You fancy you are the only champions of Protestantism. Do not become its murderers.

Glory to Christ, glory to his Word, is the watchword of the Apostles and of the Reformer — and it shall be ours!

2

CHRIST'S PERSON

IT WAS NOT ONLY Christ's Word, but Christ's Person, which Calvin, following John and Paul, desired to magnify in his life and in his death. Dwelling habitually as in his presence, he contemplated Jesus, loved, and adored him. He desired to make him known, and loudly gave glory before the world to his holy humanity and his perfect divinity.

At the present time there is a great crowd on the face of the earth that does the same. Christ's divinity was boldly proclaimed at the Revival.[1] It is thought that it was too exclusively asserted, at the expense of his humanity; accordingly,

[1] See p. 15

some persons, in these days, have put the Saviour's humanity in stronger relief; wishing, by this means, to render service to theology and practical Christianity.

I think, however, that, if others have inclined too much to the right, these lean too much to the left, when they teach that the everlasting Word, which is God, renounced, on becoming man, all the attributes, metaphysical as well as moral, which constitute the divinity; so that, for a long time, indeed, until his baptism, Christ knew not that he was the Son of God.

I shall enter into no discussion; I shall simply quote Scripture. Paul says, 'In him dwells all the fullness of the Godhead bodily.' And Calvin, explaining this passage, dwells upon it, and exclaims, 'God is in Christ wholly. In him he manifested himself fully, perfectly, and essentially.'[1]

Having quoted the Word of God, for Calvin is not my authority, I add, simply, that the system of which I am speaking does not appear to me conformable with Scripture.

[1] *Commentary on Colossians* 2:9.

But we will not linger over questions which are discussed in the church among Christians. A great work of demolition is going on at the present moment. Among the workmen employed in it, some are old, others are new. Some are full of ardour and impetuosity; others show calmness, and, perhaps, even a little lassitude. Some attack the foundations, others only the superstructure.

When we wish to pull down a house, we begin with the roof; then storey after storey is removed, until we come to the foundations, and then these are blown up, sapped, and destroyed. An analogous work is going on, in these days, against the Person of our Saviour. 'Down', they say; 'a little lower; lower still!'

First, arrayed against that throne on which he sits enrobed in glory, who, having received everything from the Father, is equal to him in his essence, are collected, in various parts of Christendom, a number of doctors similar to those who were called Semi-Arians in the fourth century, and who say, 'No doubt you come from the Father; you are even eternal, but you are not God as he is; your essence is not his; you are only like, but not equal to, him in all things.'[1] — Down a little lower!

Next comes a body, very numerous fifty or sixty years ago, but since diminished by desertions from their number, some to ascend, others to descend; a class which says, 'You are certainly a being of admirable excellence, greater than the angels and archangels; the most glorious of all creatures, but *a creature* nevertheless. There was a time when you did not exist,[2] and then God made you, created you, and called you Son.' Down lower still!

These were succeeded by others who, like many in the sixteenth century (the Socinians), said, 'Lower still! You are by nature only a man. Doubtless you have received divine wisdom from God; and, to recompense your obedience, he charged you with glorious functions; but we do not recognize in you a superhuman existence.' Lower! much lower!

---

[1] 'Εν πᾶσιν ὅμοιος ('In all things like') — Cyril of Jerusalem, AD c. 315–86.

[2] 'Ην ὅτε οὐκ ἦν ('There was a time when he was not') — *Arius*.

Up to this time, these different sectaries maintained the authority of Scripture, and the supernatural in redemption. Even the Socinians do so.[1] There are many among them who uphold the cause of a personal God, in opposition to Pantheism, and the cause of a supernatural order, in opposition to Naturalism. In so doing, they do some little good to themselves; and why should we not hope to see them one day united in the same spirit to maintain the whole revelation of God?

But there is no stopping here. Do you not hear the tumult in the world? Do you not see those bands hurrying and crowding round the lofty, perfect, divine stature of Christ? They swarm round it, striking it with their hammers and their pickaxes, kicking at it, and beating it with their fists. They are trying to break it, to pull it down, and they exclaim, 'Down lower! Much lower still!'

---

[1] *Christus a mortuis excitatus, profectus est in cœlum* (Christ, being raised from the dead, went into heaven) — *Racovian Catechism*, on Christ's Office as Priest (*De Munere Christi Sacerdotale*).

Foremost are the Rationalists, who assert the spotless moral purity of the Founder of Christianity, but deny everything supernatural — 'Lower! Down, down!'

Then come others, and among them a celebrated French author,[1] gifted with an admirable style, and sometimes with rare impartiality, who changes the gospel history into a kind of tragic idyll, whose hero is at first an amiable shepherd on the shores of the Lake of Galilee, and then a fanatic, who imprudently exposes himself to death in Jerusalem, after employing deceit and falsehood, in order to save men.

A superficial crowd of admirers surround this new prophet of Pantheism, and in their turn assail the everlasting gospel. 'Lower', they say, 'much lower!'

Then come the last, who place Christ lower than all the rest. It had been said and published in several places that one of them, speaking from the pulpit, had placed Jesus below Judas; but he

---

[1] Ernest Renan (1823–92) who, in his *Life of Jesus* (*Vie de Jesus*), 1863, gave a purely naturalistic account of the life of Christ.

has contradicted it, and affirmed that he merely said that the sacrifice of Zwingli, who died on the battlefield of Kappel, was greater than that of Jesus Christ. Assuredly this was saying quite enough. 'Lower, lower', they cry, 'lower still!'

What do you say, fellow-Christians, to these outrages? Do you think that Jesus received any greater when 'they spat in his face and buffeted him'? Alas! he is still in this nineteenth century the despised one of whom Isaiah speaks. My dear friends, let us confess his eternal divinity before all men. The more obstinately this is denied, the more boldly ought it to be proclaimed. 'Whoever refuses, and remains with his mouth shut', says Calvin, 'banishes himself from the house of God.'[1]

And you insensate destroyers! What are you doing? Wretched men, you are throwing down the only building that can shelter a poor soul disturbed by the power of sin and the bereavements of life — Cease your guilty labours! What would happen were there no more faith in the Saviour on earth? Then there would be no

[1] *Commentary on Matthew* 10:32.

Christ, no God, no peace, no everlasting life. Nothing but annihilation, according to you — nothing but death and hell.

But why should not he that is labouring hard to destroy the temple find a refuge in it some day? We ourselves, and many of our contemporaries, had learnt to honour Jesus only as the first of creatures, but God made the scales fall from our eyes, and we saw the divine and eternal glory of the Son shine forth in the Word. Why should not the grace of God call to repentance those who now speak against the Son of man? — Have you not said, O Saviour, that it shall be forgiven them?

It is true that in order to open the eyes that are closed, a servant of God is needed — one invested by him with great faith. Oh! if Calvin, that doctor of our forefathers, could appear, he who loved to place himself, full of praise and adoration, before the Man-God, and to contemplate his glory, to whom Jesus was both Saviour and Friend, would that he could make his mighty voice heard among our paltry discussions! I seem to see his pale face, his slender frame, appearing in the midst of the assemblies, discussions, and conversations, which are now taking place in Paris and London, in Holland, Germany, and Geneva. I see his majestic but stern forehead sorrowfully frowning; that keen and usually serene look growing sad; and I hear that gentle but firm and piercing voice saying, 'No! Jesus Christ is not a newly-made God; he was before all time, and his glory is eternal.'[1] 'The divine majesty, which the Son has always possessed, dwelt also in the human flesh which he had assumed. Though he lowered himself from the highest degree of honour to the lowest of all ignominy, he could not renounce his divinity.'[2] 'If we have Christ, we possess the true and eternal God.'[3]

But, my friends, why need we call Calvin back from the grave? Scripture says, 'In the beginning was the Word, and the Word was with God, and the Word was God'; and we believe Scripture. Christ himself has said, 'I and my Father are one:

[1] *Commentary on John* 1:14 and 7:46.
[2] *Commentary on Philippians* 2:6, 7.
[3] *Commentary on 1 John* 5:20.

all men should honour the Son even as they honour the Father.' And we will obey him. Glory to the Son, to the God-Man! Hosanna!

3

CHRIST'S GRACE

To the glory of the Word and the glory of the Person of Christ is joined the glory of his grace. Calvin knew that grace alone had saved him, that an inward miracle of God alone had converted him. He said to his contemporaries:

> Although I was so obstinately given over to the superstitions of Popery that it was truly difficult to drag me out of such a deep mire, God subdued me by a sudden conversion, and softened my heart which, considering my age, was far too hardened in those things. By his secret providence [his hidden action in the heart] God made me turn the rein another way, and I was straightway

inflamed with so great a desire to advance in the knowledge of true piety, that I merely trifled with my other studies.'[1]

Thus you see how Calvin's heart burns for the grace that saved him. He ascribes no part of his conversion to himself; he claims no merit. To him belongs the hardness of heart, to God alone the power and the love that break it. He is now 'inflamed' for grace. Adoration of Christ, on account of his free salvation, is at all times and in all places the fundamental note of all the harmonies he constructs.

Calvin was not slow to perceive that, according to the teaching of the Popes, the natural powers of man have not been corrupted by the Fall, but only weakened, so that man might still have some power to save himself. He saw that from this Pelagianism or semi-Pelagianism proceeded all the errors of Popery — good works, meritorious penances, human expiations, indulgences, the merits of the saints, all (in short) that is substituted for the fullness of grace. And against

[1] Calvin's Preface to his *Commentary on the Psalms*.

these errors and many others he set up the great truth: All salvation comes by the grace of Christ.

'What!' some may say, 'are you as ready to subscribe to all that Calvin said about grace and predestination as you are to profess all that is written in the Bible?' No! we place no doctor in the same rank as the prophets of God. Calvin was, perhaps, too systematic; the scholastic spirit which then prevailed, and from which he endeavoured to escape, still had some hold upon him.

As it is so difficult for man to preserve the balance between the divine and the human element, to use a theological term, the divine and the human factor, the Reformer, called to purify the church from human encroachments, may have, I will not say, *excluded* the human element, but partially *obscured* it. But we are not disciples of Calvin, but of Christ.

'Good!' you say. 'Now, therefore, we are authorized to reject that doctrine of predestination, according to which God determines certain persons to do evil and to persevere in it.' A great mistake, my friends. Calvin never said that; he even taught the very opposite, and severely chided the men who professed such doctrines.

'O mockers!' he said to them, 'Know that the wicked, far from obeying the will of God by doing evil, overthrow that divine will as much as in them lies. Our perdition comes from the sin of our flesh, and not from God.'[1]

Calvin taught, not that God predestines men to evil, but that he destines the men who do evil, and persevere in it, to receive the punishment due to their disobedience. A Christian minister, who is not regarded as a Calvinist, has composed a remarkable sermon on that well-known verse of the Proverbs, 'The LORD hath made all things for himself; yes, even the wicked for the day of evil' (*Prov.* 16:4). And as people have more indulgence for the modern preacher than for the one of the sixteenth century, I recommend you to read his discourse before you condemn Calvin. You will observe how forcibly that philosophical and Christian spirit supports the immutable decree which makes the day of evil the inheritance of

[1] *Institutes*, II.1.

the wicked, and shows that the correlation between sin and suffering is necessary and eternal.[1]

You persist, and say, 'But did not Calvin teach that God predestined some to salvation, and others to condemnation?' Yes, this proposition is to be found in the *Institutes*. But observe, however, that, if the latter are appointed to condemnation because of their revolt against God's will, there is nothing in it contrary to Scripture, nor even to right reason. Do not allow yourselves to be led astray by the phantoms which the word 'predestination' conjures up. If man fell in Eden, it was, as Calvin teaches, through his own fault. If man sins now, it is because he wishes to do so. 'It is of his own will', he says, 'that man is stripped of the righteousness which God had given him. It is of his own will that he gave himself up to Satan. It is of his own will that he is lost.'[2]

[1] Alexandre Vinet, *Nouveaux Discours* (1841), p. 36.
[2] *Sponte in exitium se præcipitem dedit* (of his own accord he plunged himself headlong into destruction) — *Consensus Genevensis*, 1552.

Yet Calvin was also a philosopher and possessed (as we have said) a systematic mind. He could not understand how anything could take place in the world without God's will. 'Why', he said, of the Fall, or of anything else, 'why does God permit it, if he does not will it?'

But does Calvin intend stopping at this obscure and metaphysical standpoint? Quite the contrary. With all his strength he diverts from it those whom he addresses. He says, 'Let us contemplate, in the corrupt nature of man, the cause of his condemnation — for there it is evident — rather than look for it in the predestination of God, where it is hidden and utterly incomprehensible.' And, employing a very striking expression, he tells those who refuse to follow this advice, 'The desire to know these things [predestination] is a kind of mania.'[1] And this idea, the study and contemplation of which he describes as a delirium, a mania — this has been called Calvin's favourite idea, his theology; in short, Calvinism. Can anything stranger be imagined?

[1] *Institutes*, III.23.8.

Follow the Reformer's advice, my Christian friends. Setting aside what is 'utterly incomprehensible', what people only think about in moments of delirium, cling to what is 'evident', that is to say, that man fell by his own fault, and is, therefore, condemned by his own fault. We must believe that it is we who are guilty. We must thus justify Calvin from the vulgar and unjust accusations that have been circulating against him for three centuries.

Do you desire to know what is the idea of the great doctor on this point — what, in his opinion, is the revelation of Scripture? He declares, with Paul, with Jesus Christ, with the whole Bible, that the redemption of believers has its foundation in an eternal counsel of the love of God. 'If we are asked', he says, 'why God has called us to the participation of the gospel; why he does us so much good every day; why he opens heaven to us . . . we must always recur to this answer: Because "He has chosen us before the foundation of the world."'[1]

[1] *Commentary on Ephesians* 1:4.

Grace, a grace of Christ, without beginning or end, which saves completely: that is Christ's gift to all those whom the Father gives him. At the sight of this ineffable gift, Calvin glorifies and magnifies the Saviour. O grace, glorious for Christ, and saving for men! Grace, which abases us, and then exalts; which, taking away all human merit, produces the profoundest humility in him whom it saves; and which, revealing God to him as being from all eternity the Author of his salvation, fills his heart with the sweetest joy and the firmest assurance. Glory to his grace!

There was, however, a divine grace which Calvin loved to contemplate as much as the eternal love of the Father: it was the death of the Son. He delighted to place himself before the cross. 'My triumph and my glory', he said, 'is in the cross of the Son of God. O death, full of ignominy and reproach! O cross, which men abhor, and God has cursed, in you I glory! . . . In you I find perfect blessedness!'[1]

Is that what the world says? Is that the language of modern Protestantism?

[1] *Commentary on Galatians* 6:14.

'We do not want to be saved by the merit of another', says the world. 'We do not want to be washed in blood.'

'What!' say our Reformers, in reply; 'What! Do you think the Everlasting One can make a law, and that law not be fulfilled? If the law is transgressed, must not God necessarily sanction it by punishing the trangressor?' Were it not so, there would be no holiness in God; that is to say, there would be no God. Your conscience, O sinner, declares it to you. It cries aloud to you that, by sinning, you have offended the Most High; and the consciousness of your sin draws forth those heavy groans. Hear how Calvin consoles: 'O you who are full of fear and trembling, because you have not yet reposed and rested in Jesus Christ, know that he is our peace. He became guilty for us before the judgment seat of the Father; he endured the penalty to which we were condemned; he received on himself all our condemnation.'[1]

O anxious, troubled soul, for there may, perhaps, be one such before me now, what a

[1] *Commentary on Romans* 5:1.

grace is the grace of the cross! Christ has ransomed you from the curse of the law.

Depart, then, in peace. Leap with joy, O troubled soul! You are washed, you are saved by the blood of Emmanuel! Glory to the grace that Christ purchased for us on the cross!

The great Reformer continues his march. Guided by the hand of God, he has found the grace of Christ in eternity; he has found it at Calvary. He now goes further, and discovers it acting with power, and alone, in the hearts of the children of God.

But the strength of the natural man (some will say), the light of the heathens, their luminous thoughts! 'Yes', answers Calvin, picturesquely, 'if a man is overtaken by a thunderstorm, in the middle of a common, at night, he will see a long way round him by the help of the lightning; but it will only be for an instant, and will be of no use to show him the right road, for the flash vanishes so quickly that he is once more enveloped in darkness before he can catch sight of the path.'[1] The noblest impulses of the wisest

[1] *Institutes*, II.2.

men are, in the Reformer's opinion, only gentle knocks on the door of the temple of light, in spite of which the temple remains closed. But, 'The Holy Spirit', he tells us, 'opens the door to us, so that we may enter and lay hold of the treasures of heaven.'[1]

But these objectors insist: We meet (as Calvin did in his time) with men who believe in the Holy Spirit, but in whose judgment the grace of God and the will of man are two allied powers, which, uniting their action, gain the victory, and accomplish conversion. Calvin studied this system. His penetrating mind discovered that one of the allies, the grace of God, was, in this system, only a remote power, operating upon all, and mostly without success; while the other, the human will, was the proximate, specific, and favourite cause, the one that put a difference between man saved and man lost. The great teacher of modern times did not hesitate between the creature and the Creator. With Paul, he ascribed all the victory to the grace of God alone. 'Yet not I', says Paul, 'but the grace of God which was with me.'

[1] *Commentary on Acts* 2:17.

'We can do nothing', says Calvin, 'unless by a supernatural grace of God. It is God who gives the will, it is God who gives the power.' And, ravished at the sight of the triumphs which the sovereign power of God promises, he exclaims in his striking manner: 'Here is the sword to cut down all our pride! Here is the real artillery to batter down all our haughtiness!'

And we, too, O Lord, all feeble as we are, in this our day give glory to your grace! We declare before the church, before the world, before you, O God, and before your angels, that if you had not come to us, we should never have gone to you. If you had not given us the will to be saved, we never should have been saved. You have said: 'You have not chosen me, but I have chosen you.' — We believe it, O Christ, and we magnify your love and your election! Glory to your grace!

4

CHRIST'S LIFE

'BUT DID THE REFORMATION and the Reformers care for nothing but doctrines?', you may ask. No, they glorified the life of Christ, and life for Christ.

It is not the works of the law that make the Christian, say all the Reformers; it is not baptism, confirmation, admission to the Lord's table; it is not the upright life that may be found even among heathens, external works, the profession of the lips, gestures, movements of eyes, hands, or feet; it is not even an orthodox but dead faith in the divinity of Christ and his work.

No, what makes the real Christian is the new birth, the new creature, the new life: it is Christ living in us. All the Reformers said this; but Calvin dwelt upon it with a power peculiarly his own.

Even now we greatly need the teaching of the Reformer. The most general heresy of our age, and, indeed, of all ages, consists in unwillingness to be regenerated. There is a league against life. 'Leave us', say some, 'in the pleasures of the world.' 'Leave us', say others, 'in our own righteousness.' 'Leave us', says a third class, 'in our orthodoxy, in our good works, in our committees.' 'Leave us', they all say, 'just as we are. Why should we change?' Why? Listen to Calvin's answer: 'Because, in the kingdom of Christ, it is only the new man that has any vigour, and is to be taken into account.' And here is Christ's answer: 'Except a man be born again, he cannot see the kingdom of God.'

If you listen at Geneva or elsewhere to those who do not know Calvin (I do not speak of mere libellers, but of men worthy in other respects), they will say: 'Calvin's theology is only ideas, dogmas, formulae.' I reply that it is the very opposite. In Calvin's eyes the Reformation was essentially the renovation of the individual, and, consequently, the renovation of Christendom.

The new birth of the individual and of the church is the distinctive characteristic of Calvin's doctrine. One of our most celebrated contemporaries in Germany, that eloquent orator and profound lawyer, F. J. Stahl, who professed an exaggerated Lutheranism, said: 'Calvin has brought a new principle into Protestantism.' Indeed! What is this new principle imported by Calvin into the Reformation after Luther? An extreme Lutheran shall inform us. Stahl continues: 'This principle is the glorification of God by the real and complete sovereignty of his Word in the life of Christendom. The Word of God is not only, according to Calvin, an original document of Christianity: it is the constant discourse of an ever-present God. The church ought to be filled with this holy presence, which admits of no impurity.'[1] What noble homage paid to Calvin by one of his most illustrious adversaries!

[1] Friedrich Julius Stahl (1802–61), *Die Lutherische Kirche und die Union* (1860).

But it is not only in the heart that Christ must be glorified; it is (according to Calvin) in the whole life. Let us visit the Geneva of the sixteenth century; let us call upon the Reformer. Enter his house, and take note of its simplicity.

Here is his furniture: three bedsteads, three tables, a desk, a high-backed chair, and a dozen stools, 'some good, some bad', says the inventory.[1] His poverty and disinterestedness glorified Christ. Knock at his door at the first gleam of daylight, and you will find him at work; return at midnight, and he is there still. His unceasing labour glorified Christ.

Listen to his preaching, his conferences, his lessons, his conversations with his colleagues, with the members of his flock and with the numerous refugees continually arriving; look at his letters, and his books, which are circulated throughout Christendom: they all glorified Christ.

[1] 'Tant bonnes que méchantes': La Demeure de Calvin ('Some good, some bad': Calvin's House). *Mémoires d'Archéologie de Genéve*, vol. x.

Observe him in his care of souls, in his visits to the sick, to the stranger, to the magistrates, and to the poor. He ascends to the garret; he is not contented with the city, he traverses the suburbs, and recalls the dissolute to their duty. Pastor of all Christendom, he was particularly the pastor of Geneva. 'The Church of Geneva is so dear to my heart', he said, 'that I could give my life for it.' There is no church which he does not direct; no minister whom he does not encourage; no prisoner and martyr whom he does not console. His whole life glorifies the Lord.

And that glory of Christ, which shone forth in his person, shone forth also in the life of the church which he had formed. Of this we have eye-witnesses. An eminent Christian, the first, perhaps, after Calvin, in the Reformed Church, John Knox, who had lived some years at Geneva, speaking of this city to one of his friends in England, said: 'I could have wished, yea, and cannot cease to wish, that it might please God to guide and conduct yourself where, I neither fear nor shame to say, is the most perfect school of

Christ that ever was on earth since the days of the Apostles. In other places I confess Christ to be truly preached; but manners and religion so sincerely reformed I have not yet seen in any other place beside.'

Knox was so affected by it, that, when he believed the Reformation established in Scotland, he was seized with an almost irresistible desire to return to Geneva, and end his days in the midst of this flock, 'among whom he had lived with such quietness of conscience and contentment of heart'.

That is not all: Calvin glorified Christ even by his death, to use Paul's expression. In February 1564, he was seized with a sudden illness in the pulpit, and was obliged to come tottering down, yet he continued his labours in his study, and replied to the friends who tried to dissuade him from it: 'When the Lord cometh, would you have him find me idle?'

When, on the 27 March, wishing even to the last to give honour to whom honour is due, he had himself carried to the Council, and there, rising from the low seat on which they had placed him, he stood cap in hand, and trembling all over, and with broken voice, he humbly thanked their lordships for the kindness they had shown him: did not Calvin glorify Jesus Christ by his humility?

When he went to St Peter's[1] at Easter for his last communion, when, at the sight of the broken bread and of the consecrated cup presented to him by Theodore Beza, the love of Christ who died for him so struck him and so lightened up his face that all the congregation beheld with extreme consolation their dying pastor so serene and so joyful, did he not glorify Jesus Christ?

When, on the 27 April, his chamber was filled with the syndics and councillors, who had desired to offer him their last homage; when the Reformer, thinner, paler, and more trembling than usual, sat up in his bed, and protested before God that he had endeavoured to teach the Word purely; when he reminded them that it was God alone who upheld cities and kingdoms, and said: 'Look to him who has established you, praying

---

[1] Geneva's principal church, the *Cathédrale Saint-Pierre*.

him to guide you by his Holy Spirit', did he not glorify Jesus Christ?

When he assembled the ministers next day, and said to them: 'I exhort you, brethren, to show after my death the same zeal in the discharge of your functions as you have done hitherto, and never to lose heart, being persuaded that the Lord will preserve this church from all danger', did he not glorify Jesus Christ?

When addressing his friend Farel for the last time, he wrote: 'I expect from hour to hour that I shall breathe my last . . . But it is enough for me to live and die in Christ; for he is my gain in life and in death', did he not glorify Jesus Christ?

When, at the approach of the last moments, smarting under acute pain, his life was a continual suffering, a continual prayer, and when he exclaimed: 'I am silent because you have done it!', and when at another time he said: 'O Lord, you are crushing me; but it is from your hand, and that is enough', did he not glorify Jesus Christ?

Assuredly Christ was glorified by this life and this death! Glory, glory to the Saviour!

And now, to what does my duty urge me? To entreat you to magnify Christ as Paul did, as Calvin did, and as so many of the servants of God, the most illustrious as well as the most obscure, have done. But I feel what little right I have to appeal to you. At first I hesitated to enter this pulpit, not only because of my diminished strength, but still more because I felt that the task to which I was this day summoned, was far beyond me. I said to myself: Have the great truths which I must announce sufficient power over me?

And am I not far inferior to many among those whom I must conjure to receive and proclaim them? I took up their cause against myself; I wished to be silent, and exclaimed with Jeremiah: 'Ah, Lord God, behold I cannot speak'; and with David: 'Oh that I had wings like a dove, then would I fly away and be at rest.'

But a voice from heaven sounded through my heart; overpowering recollections came over me. I said, I will go up into that pulpit once more, perhaps for the last time. I have, therefore, come into the midst of you; I have said the words that I was desired to say. May God cast the mantle of his mercies over the weaknesses and the excesses of my discourse.

But since I am in this place, I will not leave it without making one last and solemn appeal on behalf of the Lord: Manifest the glory of Jesus Christ. It is the time to set it in the light of day. Manifest it by your humility, your meekness, your charity, but also with firmness and courage. It is not our own glory that we should care about, but the glory of him who has saved us. How can you expect from him an incorruptible crown in heaven, if you have not placed one upon his head here below? When you appear before his throne on the great day, do you wish to hear him say, 'You did not serve me, honour me, magnify me on earth: Depart, I do not know you'?

To work then, Christians, to work! If any cast-down and despairing soul is comforted, because you have taught it to know the compassion of Christ, Christ will be glorified. If any dead and lost soul, living without God in the world, is converted and saved, because you have taught it to know the cross of Christ, Christ will be glorified. If any soul, tossed on the waves of doubt and driven to and fro by the winds of unbelief, finds faith and peace, because you have taught it to know the true Rock, Christ will be glorified.

Higher, Christians, higher! *Excelsior!* Let the church ascend to the heights on which Calvin, nay, rather, on which Christ has placed it. Let the commemoration of these days revive in all our flocks, not legal enactments, but faith, profound scriptural knowledge, ardent attachment to truth, sanctification in the Lord, compassion for the afflicted, a spirit of devotion and sacrifice, indefatigable activity, and a love for Jesus Christ, of which the great Reformer has left us such an example.

Let there be for every one of us in this day of death a real resurrection. 'Let what is cool come to be warmed', as Calvin says, 'for a little fire will go out, unless it be fostered by blowing it and by adding fresh fuel.'

Come, Lord, add fresh fuel and blow upon the fire, since your breath alone gives flame and life. Breathe upon these half-consumed embers, and may a heavenly fire burn in your people!

'Baptize us with the Spirit and with fire.' And despite all those floods of icy water which imprudent workers are now pouring on the altar you have kindled upon earth, 'Let the house of Jacob become a fire, and the house of Joseph become a flame'; and let all of us, children of the Reformation and of the gospel, be lights in the world, and manifest in it from this day forward your Word, your Person, your Grace, your Life, your Glory, O Jesus Christ, King of the church, our Lord and our God!

OTHER CALVIN TITLES FROM
THE BANNER OF TRUTH TRUST

Letters of John Calvin, 264 pp., paperback
Sermons on 2 Samuel 1–13, 696 pp., clothbound
Sermons on Job, 784 pp., clothbound
Sermons on the Beatitudes, 128 pp., clothbound
Sermons on Galatians, 688 pp., clothbound
Sermons on Ephesians, 728 pp., clothbound
Sermons on Timothy & Titus, 1280 pp.,
clothbound
*Truth for All Time: A Brief Outline of the
Christian Faith*, 90 pp., paperback

GENEVA SERIES COMMENTARIES
Genesis, 1088 pp., clothbound
Jeremiah & Lamentations, 5 vols., clothbound
Daniel, 808 pp., clothbound
Hosea, 544 pp., clothbound
Joel, Amos & Obadiah, 520 pp., clothbound

Jonah, Micah & Nahum, 544 pp., clothbound
Habakkuk, Zephaniah & Haggai, 416 pp.,
clothbound
Zechariah & Malachi, 720 pp., clothbound

NOTE: Calvin's *Sermons,* of which the Trust has six
volumes in print (see previous page), should be
distinguished from his *Commentaries.* Spurgeon
said of the *Sermons on Ephesians,* 'Not the same
as the exposition. The Sermons are priceless.'

'Perhaps there is no better introduction to Calvin
the Preacher than his *Sermons on the Beatitudes.*
Here is the best way to get at the essence of the
Preacher and the Pastor. The book is chock-full of
practical observations and tender exhortations to
his listeners. In these messages his heart is laid
bare before the congregation.'

'A gem of a book, an excellent introduction to
Calvin the preacher and Calvin the man.'

From reviews of SERMONS ON THE BEATITUDES
(ISBN 0 85151 934 2, 128 pp., clothbound)
on the World Wide Web.

For free illustrated catalogue please write to
THE BANNER OF TRUTH TRUST

3 Murrayfield Road,   P O Box 621, Carlisle,
Edinburgh EH12 6EL   Pennsylvania 17013,
UK   USA

www.banneroftruth.co.uk